**W9-BCX-929**

SCIENCE EXPLORER JUNIOR

JUNIOR SCIENTISTS

Experiment with Solids

by Josh Gregory

MICHIGAN

Published in the United States of America by Cherry Lake Publishing
Ann Arbor, Michigan
www.cherrylakepublishing.com

Content Editor: Robert Wolffe, EdD, Professor of Teacher Education, Bradley University, Peoria, Illinois
Reading Adviser: Cecilia Minden-Cupp, PhD, Literacy Consultant

Design and Illustration: The Design Lab

Photo Credits: Page 9, ©Morgan Lane Photography/Shutterstock, Inc.; page 15, ©Mikephotos/Dreamstime.com; page 16, ©Golden Pixels LLC/Shutterstock, Inc.; page 21, ©Irochka/Dreamstime.com; page 22, ©Marbo/Dreamstime.com; page 27, ©Phil Degginger/Alamy; page 28, ©Pazham/Dreamstime.com

Library of Congress Cataloging-in-Publication Data
Gregory, Josh.
 Junior scientists. Experiment with solids / by Josh Gregory.
   p. cm.–(Science explorer junior)
 Includes bibliographical references and index.
 ISBN-13: 978-1-60279-845-8 (lib. bdg.)
 ISBN-10: 1-60279-845-1 (lib. bdg.)
 1. Solids—Experiments—Juvenile literature. 2. Matter—Properties—Experiments—Juvenile literature. 3. Science Projects—Juvenile literature. I. Title. II. Title: Experiment with solids. III. Series.
 QC176.3.G74 2010
 531.078–dc22   2009048842

Portions of the text have previously appeared in *Super Cool Science Experiments: States of Matter* published by Cherry Lake Publishing.

Cherry Lake Publishing would like to acknowledge the work of The Partnership for 21st Century Skills. Please visit *www.21stcenturyskills.org* for more information.

Printed in the United States of America
Corporate Graphics Inc.
July 2010
CLFA07

TABLE OF CONTENTS

Let's Experiment!

Experiments are fun!

Have you ever done a science **experiment**? They can be a lot of fun! You can use experiments to learn about almost anything.

Scientists observe the world around them.

This book will help you learn how to think like a scientist. Scientists have a special way of learning new things. Some people call it the Scientific Method. This is how it often works:

- Scientists notice things. They **observe** the world around them. They ask questions about things they see, hear, taste, touch, or smell. They come up with problems they would like to solve.

A scientist makes a guess called a hypothesis.

- They gather information. They use what they already know to guess the answers to their questions. This kind of guess is called a **hypothesis**.

- Then they test their ideas. They perform experiments or build models. They watch and write down what happens. They learn from each new test.

Scientists perform experiments to test their ideas.

• They think about what they learned and reach a **conclusion**. This means they come up with an answer to their question. Sometimes they conclude that they need to do more experiments!

Conclusion

When a scientist figures out the answer to his question, he has reached a conclusion.

Can you name three solids in this classroom?

We will think like scientists to learn more about solids. Solids are everywhere. Almost everything you touch is a solid. Your desk at school is a solid. So is your toothbrush. Have you ever had questions about solids? What makes them different from liquids and gases? What gives them their shapes? What happens when you heat them? We can answer these questions and more by doing experiments. Are you ready to be a scientist?

Mix It Up

Think about the states of matter when sipping a fizzy drink!

Solids, liquids, and gases are all around us. Picture a glass of fizzy soda. The glass is a solid. The soda is a liquid. The bubbles have gas. Solids, liquids, and gases are three **states of matter**. What makes solids different from liquids and gases? You may already know that solids keep their shape. This is true unless a force acts on them.

Think about mixing two liquids. The result depends on which liquids you choose. Once mixed, they may create a new liquid. The new liquid cannot be changed back into the first two. What about solids? Is it possible to separate solids after they are mixed? Let's find out! You'll need to start with a hypothesis. Try one of these:

1. Solids can often be separated after being mixed together.
2. Solids cannot be separated after being mixed together.

Write down your hypothesis.

Wash your hands with soap and water before running this experiment. Let's get started!

Here's what you'll need:

- ½ cup banana chips
- ½ cup raisins
- ½ cup chocolate chips
- Mixing bowl

Collect your supplies.

Instructions:

1. Place the banana chips, raisins, and chocolate chips in a bowl.
2. Use your hands to mix the parts.
3. Look at the mixture. Does it look like a new substance? Can you still see the different parts? Write down your observations.

Scientists take careful notes.

Observations

4. Now try to separate your mixture. Start by removing all of the banana chips. Then take out the raisins. Now remove the chocolate chips. Did it work?

Conclusion:

Sometimes, certain solids can react with each other. An important change occurs. The original parts cannot be separated. But did you find it easy to separate your mixture? This is because many times, solid shapes do not change. They will not **bond** with other solids. This means they will not stick together in a special way. Did you prove your hypothesis?

Is it possible to separate these marbles?

Meltdown

Some liquids can be frozen to make yummy treats!

Have you ever made ice for your drinks? Did you discover that you can turn liquids into solids by freezing them? Can we also turn solids into liquids by warming them up? Let's do a simple experiment to find out. Choose a hypothesis:

1. Solids can be turned into liquids when they are heated.
2. Solids cannot be turned into liquids when they are heated.

Let's get started!

Think about what you already know about solids before choosing a hypothesis.

Hypothesis: Solids can be turned into liquids when they are heated.

Here's what you'll need:

- Small chunk of cold butter
- Chocolate chips
- Ice cube
- 3 small, microwave-safe bowls
- Microwave
- Adult helper

You'll need an adult to help test your hypothesis.

Instructions:

1. Put the ice cube in one bowl. Place the butter in the second bowl. Put the chocolate chips in the third bowl.

It won't take long to set up this experiment.

2. The microwave is your heat source. Ask an adult to microwave the ice cube for 1 minute. What happened? Write down your observations.
3. Repeat Step #2 with the butter.
4. Repeat Step #2 with the chocolate chips.

Taking notes will help you reach a conclusion.

Observations

Solid candle wax turns into a liquid when it is heated.

Conclusion:

Did the solids change into liquids? Did all three solids start to melt quickly? Did the ice cube turn into water? Did the butter totally melt? What happened to the chocolate chips? Solids can be changed into liquids using heat. Some solids need more heat than others to melt. Did the chocolate and butter melt as quickly as the ice? Did you prove your hypothesis?

Taking Up Space

Get ready to learn something special about solid water!

We've learned that a substance can be both a liquid and a solid. Think about the liquid and solid forms of a substance. Will both forms take up the same amount of space? We can do a simple experiment to find out. Start by choosing a hypothesis:

1. Liquid and solid water take up the same amount of space.
2. Liquid and solid water do not take up the same amount of space.

Let's get started!

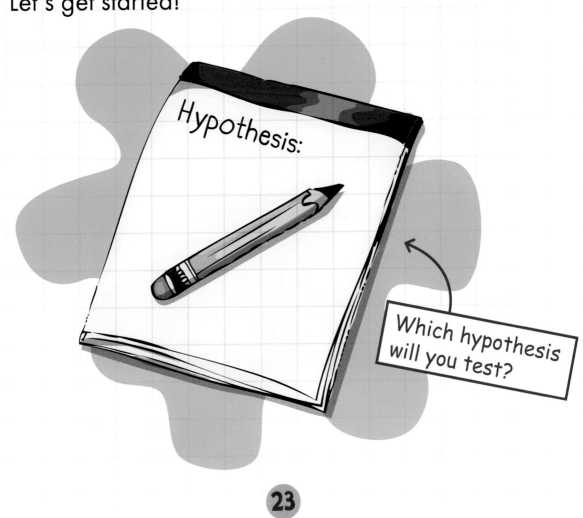

Hypothesis:

Which hypothesis will you test?

Here's what you'll need:

- Water
- Clear plastic bottle
- Marker
- Freezer

Run this experiment in your kitchen.

Instructions:

1. Fill the plastic bottle halfway with water.
2. Mark the exact water level on the bottle with the marker.
3. Put the bottle of water in the freezer. Make sure the bottle is set straight up. It should not be leaning on anything. Leave it in the freezer overnight.

4. Take the bottle out of the freezer. Compare the
   new water level to the one you marked before
   freezing.

Conclusion:

Notice the level of the ice. Is it higher than the water level you marked? This means ice takes up more space. Be careful, though. Most things do not take up more space when they freeze. They take up less space! Remember, our experiment only tested water and ice. Was your hypothesis correct?

Can you explain why this bottle of water cracked in the freezer?

Do It Yourself!

Have you thought of another hypothesis to test?

Okay, scientists! Now you know some new things about solids. You learned that solids can be turned into liquids using heat. Liquids and solids can also take up different amounts of space. You learned by using the scientific method. Now try using it to answer other questions about solids.

Can a solid be turned into a gas? Can you think of a good solid to test? How about ice? Come up with a hypothesis. Then create an experiment to find out!

What happens when ice gets really hot?

GLOSSARY

bond (BOND) hold together in a special way

conclude (kuhn-KLOOD) to make a final decision based on what you know

conclusion (kuhn-KLOO-zhuhn) a final decision, thought, or opinion

experiment (ecks-PARE-uh-ment) a scientific way to test a guess about something

hypothesis (hy-POTH-uh-sihss) a guess about what will happen in an experiment

method (METH-uhd) a way of doing something

observe (uhb-ZURV) to see something or notice things by using the other senses

states of matter (STAYTSS UHV MAT-uhr) the different forms matter can take; for example, water can be a solid (ice), a liquid (drinking water), or a gas (steam)

FOR MORE INFORMATION

BOOKS

Gaff, Jackie. *Looking at Solids, Liquids, and Gases: How Does Matter Change?* Berkeley Heights, NJ: Enslow Publishers, 2008.

Royston, Angela. *Solids, Liquids, and Gases.* Chicago: Heinemann Library, 2008.

WEB SITES

BBC—Changing state
www.bbc.co.uk/schools/ks2bitesize/science/materials/ changing_state/play.shtml
Try this fun activity, and learn more about the states of matter.

BBC—Solids and Liquids
www.bbc.co.uk/schools/ks2bitesize/science/materials/solids_ liquids/read1.shtml
Learn more about heating and cooling solids.

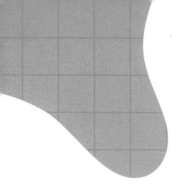

INDEX

ABOUT THE AUTHOR

Josh Gregory is an author and editor. He lives in Chicago, Illinois.